A souvenir guide

Bodiam Castle
East Sussex

Jonathan Foyle

C000226227

The Spirit of Bodiam	2
Sir Edward Dallingridge	4
Early life	6
Knight of the shire	8
Fortress or folly?	10
Threats	12
The medieval idea of a castle	14
Heraldry at Bodiam	16
Building Bodiam Castle	18
Setting	20
Shape	22
Layout	24
Exploring the Castle	26
Later History	34
Antiquarians	36
Repair and restoration	38
Ancient and modern: The pill-box	40

National Trust

The Spirit of Bodiam

Bodiam is the quintessential English castle, an echo from distant and very different times.

Another world

The castle survives physically as a moated ruin within the Rother valley, but its spirit resides in its power to capture your imagination and allow you to 'look into another world'. Reactions are distinct and personal: for some, the place evokes imagery of medieval knights; for others, it is the ultimate 'bucket and spade' castle.

A turbulent age

Bodiam Castle was built about 1380–85 by Sir Edward Dallingridge and his wife Elizabeth. They lived in a turbulent age: from the Black Death in 1348; through the protest and social upheaval it provoked; to the royal disputes that led to the Wars of the Roses.

Throughout the second half of the fourteenth century, England was at war with France, which brought Sir Edward prestige and wealth. Sir Edward was a soldier of fortune in north-western France from 1367, Knight of the Shire of Sussex after 1379 and Warden of London in 1392, a promotion made by King Richard II (reigned 1377–99). As a servant of King Richard, Dallingridge reached the highest circles of English society. Bodiam Castle opens a window onto late fourteenth-century England, the world of Chaucer.

A romantic relic

The castle is an exceptional survival, both as a work of architecture and for its medieval setting. In contrast, its interiors fell into ruin without any record surviving of how they were organised.

Reappraised as a romantic relic of archaeological curiosity in the eighteenth century, the castle was repaired by a series of owners, most notably Lord Curzon, who owned Bodiam from 1917. He bequeathed it to the National Trust in 1926, since when numerous discoveries and reinterpretations have thrown new light on the building and its site.

Opposite below **The ivy-clad Bodiam Castle as romantic relic**

Opposite above A Dallingridge in combat

Below The epitome of the medieval warrior: the tomb effigy of the Black Prince, son of Edward III, in Canterbury Cathedral

Sir Edward Dallingridge

Bodiam Castle represents the ambition of one man, the warrior knight Sir Edward Dallingridge.

Family background

Dallingridge was born around 1346 to wealthy parents. His father Roger was a royal forester whose family was named after Dalling Ridge in the Ashdown Forest in Sussex, but Roger Dallingridge also served as a man-at-arms for Edward III in the Scottish campaign of 1336. Roger's first wife – and Edward's mother – was Alice Radingen, one of three daughters of Sir John de Radington, whose family held considerable tracts of land in Sussex and the East Midlands. When Sir John died in 1350, Sir Roger and Alice inherited five Sussex manors. Their principal seat was at Fletching, 25 miles west of Bodiam. There, they raised their son Edward, who would build Bodiam Castle.

Left This magnificent tomb brass in Fletching church may commemorate Sir Edward's father, Roger Dallingridge, and his mother, Alice Radingen

A world at war

Through a life spent in south-east England and north-western France in the latter half of the fourteenth century, Edward Dallingridge experienced the turbulence of war, plague and social unrest. In common with the majority of medieval Europeans, whose spiritual beliefs were determined by the church, he felt the doctrinal promise of heaven and threat of hell. If a war were to be fought, it would be a righteous one.

Edward was born into the so-called 'Hundred Years War', which stretched from 1337 to 1453. English monarchs were attempting to regain the duchy of Aquitaine on the west coast of France, which had been inherited by Edward III, but lost to France in 1337. King Edward declared war and assumed the status of King of France in 1340, changing the English royal arms so that the French fleur-de-lis was quartered with the English lions. This remained the basis of the English royal arms until 1800.

Above Edward III, who devoted much of his life attempting to regain his French inheritance

Left Edward III's coat of arms, which quarters the French fleur-de-lis with the English lions

Early life

Edward Dallingridge's probable birth year of 1346 saw the Battle of Crécy, at which Edward III routed a French army, supported by Genoese crossbowmen nursing damp weapons and damper spirits. The English used longbows whose strings they had kept dry.

The thunder of cannons

The Italian chronicler Giovanni Villani records an important innovation at Crécy: 'The English guns cast iron balls by means of fire... They made a noise like thunder and caused much loss in men and horses.'

Below A replica of the probably fifteenth-century cannon which was dredged out of the Bodiam moat

Patriotism and profit

Heralding the dawn of cannon-fire, Crécy proved a defining moment in the Hundred Years War, and it led to the English capture of Calais the following year. The favoured tactic was the *chevauchée,* a raid on horseback to despoil enemy territory by fire and ransacking. This guerrilla tactic offered a solution to the dearth of available soldiers following the Black Death of 1348–52. The political chaos bred opportunism for a band of English warriors of diverse origins. Though they proclaimed patriotism, their common goal was profit from looting and ransoms. At the Battle of Poitiers in 1356, the new King of France John II was taken captive, and brought to England, where he was kept at numerous locations including Sussex. What effect did all this violence have on the imagination of a ten-year-old boy? We can only guess, but at just thirteen Dallingridge experienced his first military campaign with King Edward III's forces at Rheims.

Left above Sir Robert Knollys leading a raid into France. Dallingridge fought under this notoriously rapacious warrior and in gratitude placed the Knollys coat of arms and crest on Bodiam's Postern Tower

Opposite The Battle of Crécy, at which the English archers (on the right) defeated the French and Italian crossbowmen (on the left)

The spoils of war

After 1361 Edward's father Roger Dallingridge became a supporter of the politically powerful Richard, Earl of Arundel, whose seat of Arundel Castle lay in west Sussex. This was an important family tie, on which Edward capitalized when he established himself in the county. But he had other patrons. During a number of French campaigns he joined Sir Robert Knollys, a notoriously brutal head of a 'Free Company' or mercenary band. The war continued to offer enormous spoils for knights, and both Knollys's and Dallingridge's careers were forged by it. Knollys's booty funded a moated, castle-like residence at Derval (Loire-Atlantique), which Dallingridge presumably visited, as Bodiam resembled Derval.

Knight of the shire

In 1364 Edward Dallingridge married Elizabeth Wardieu (c.1347–83), daughter of John Wardieu of Bodiam. Through this union, the manor and lands in Bodiam village came to the Dallingridge family.

It is possible that a moat already existed on the site of the castle, but the Dallingridges' residence was probably Court Lodge to its north (see p.10). The couple had a daughter called Margaret, whose namesake St Margaret of Antioch was – like St George – a slayer of dragons. Perhaps she was named for a soldier's daughter. A son called John followed, who inherited his father's career as a knighted royal man-at-arms.

A royal servant

Dallingridge can have seen little of his children, as he was frequently abroad when war flared in the later 1360s. In 1377 Dallingridge returned to England, having inherited his father-in-law's estates. By that year, Edward the Black Prince and the formidable King Edward III were both dead. There followed the vulnerable reign of the young Richard II (reigned 1377–99), under whom Dallingridge developed a career in public office. As a warrior and tactician he made an apt public and royal servant. For in the same year – 1377 – a Franco-Castilian fleet mounted raids on Rye and New Winchelsea, which burned those towns.

Left The Westminster portrait of Richard II was painted in the 1390s, when Dallingridge served in the king's court

Dallingridge joined a successful *chevauchée* attack on the port of Cherbourg, which surrendered to the English in June 1378. By then Dallingridge was recorded in possession of Bodiam. Tantalisingly, it was also in 1378 that the city of Canterbury built substantial defences against the French under the guidance of the royal architect Henry Yevele, of which Westgate remains. This is England's largest medieval urban gateway, its massiveness and early gun ports demonstrating how serious the threat was considered.

Dallingridge must have watched all this very closely, for it was his business. When he became Knight of the Shire of Sussex in 1379, he represented the county in Parliament.

By May 1380 he was a commissioner examining the state of the nation and the expenses of the king's household. In this, the year of his father's death, his attention was demanded by the vulnerable coastal towns of Sussex.

A grievous wound

On 5 July 1380 he became surveyor of the coastal defences of New Winchelsea, which was attacked in the same month, when its security proved wanting. Dallingridge was personally involved in driving back these French raids, notably fending off a strike on Eastbourne in 1380. He paid a heavy price in September that year:

'[Edward Dallingridge] … by the king and council commanded to abide upon the defence of the seashore of Sussex against the king's enemies, is grievously wounded at Bourne co. Sussex.'

Despite this wound, he was sufficiently recovered to take responsibility for the fortification of Rye in 1382, a task that continued until at least 1385. By this time, he had secured permission for a fair and market at Bodiam, indicating that the family presence was being consolidated here. The church at Bodiam was also being rebuilt in 1382.

Left Dallingridge's daughter was named after the dragon slayer, St Margaret of Antioch

Right The massive Westgate was built to defend Canterbury against the French

Fortress or folly?

Dallingridge represented Sussex in the parliament that ran from 20 October to 6 December 1385. The day it opened, he was granted a licence to fortify Bodiam Castle (see quote below).

Bodiam gets royal planning permission
'that he may strengthen with a wall of stone and lime, and crenellate and may construct and make into a castle his manor house of Bodyham, near the sea, in the County of Sussex, for the defence of the adjacent country, and the resistance to our enemies...'

Was the mention of 'our enemies' an explicit rationale for Bodiam Castle, or was it symbolic, implying the fortress was a chivalric ornament of the realm? Importantly, Dallingridge hadn't retired from active service when he began

building. He remained a soldier abroad on French campaigns into the late 1380s, serving as Captain of Brest (Brittany) during 1386–7. In April 1390 he was made a commissioner both of the conclusion of a truce between England and France, and a surveyor of the castles and fortresses of Calais and Picardy. To the end of his life, the Plantagenet war against the Valois monarchs of France remained unsettled, while the English Channel stayed a war zone. It was a war that his son also fought in.

The medieval moated enclosure
Well east of the old Roman Road, to the north-east of the medieval church, is an oval moated enclosure. It was probably responsible for the crescent-shaped string of fishponds that were inherited as a garden setting for the castle, interrupted by the insertion of the north arm of the castle's moat.

There has been much speculation about the origin and demise of this site and its relationship to the castle. The most recent theory is that it was the dwelling of Richard Wardieu, younger brother of Nicholas, who held the manor until c.1330. The archaeological evidence suggests that it was abandoned and so collapsed, though some of its Flemish bricks and clay tiles were used in constructing the castle. While it was being built, the Dallingridges probably lived on the site of Court Lodge, to the north.

Opposite St Giles Church, Bodiam. The moated enclosure (now gone) lay just to the north

Above Bodiam was designed both to deter and impress

Threats

In the years leading to the construction of Bodiam Castle, the French weren't the only threat to English knights. The personal vulnerability and grievance Dallingridge must have felt at Eastbourne in 1380 coincided with the violent social unrest since called the 'Peasants' Revolt'.

The Peasants' Revolt was ostensibly in response to the poll tax, but also manifested changing attitudes in society. In 1381 Richard II was challenged at Blackheath by the rebel Wat Tyler and his followers, who had amassed as 'Men of Kent', coming perhaps from the Maidstone area, and certainly not far from Bodiam. Having stormed the Tower of London, the rebels shockingly decapitated Simon Sudbury, Archbishop of Canterbury and Chancellor of England. This south-eastern uprising spilled into Sussex and had the makings of civil war, a deeply disturbing prospect.

Challenging the crown

Dallingridge mounted a rebellion of his own against a member of the royal family. It originated in 1372, when John of Gaunt (the third surviving son of Edward III) had been granted land in Sussex, in Pevensey and also Ashdown, from which Dallingridge's family had come. The sudden imbalance in power created unhappiness amongst the populace Dallingridge represented in parliament. From 1377, he and other Sussex landowners had waged a campaign of intimidation against Gaunt's servants and property. When Dallingridge was tried in June

1384, he was summoned for contempt of court, as he literally threw down his gauntlet. Arundel ensured that he escaped the worst effects of justice, but his was just one of many challenges to royal authority. The parliament of 1386 saw the impeachment of Chancellor de la Pole, and powers stripped from Richard II, now aged nineteen. For now, Dallingridge was on the right side, working with Arundel to secure oaths of allegiance to the young king from the landowners of the south-east. He was rewarded with his elevation to the King's Council in May 1389, a role he fulfilled diligently.

Above **The murder of Simon Sudbury, Archbishop of Canterbury**

Opposite above **Dallingridge grew up in the shadow of the Black Death, which wiped out more than a third of the British population**

Opposite below **The dagger with which William Walworth killed the rebel leader Wat Tyler in 1381**

Disease

Disease was another lethal threat. Dallingridge had been an infant when the Black Death raged in 1348–52, killing perhaps 40% of the population. Stories of suffering, plague carts and pits must have remained rife, and the ever-present danger of 'sweating sickness' in urban areas encouraged the building of country residences. Pestilence was omnipresent.

'The deaths in Norfolk and many other counties increased to such a number that this plague seemed just as bad as the big plagues preceding it.'

The chronicler Thomas Walsingham, summer 1391

Civil disturbance

It was neither French troops nor pestilence, but civil disturbance that led to Dallingridge's last official role. At Nottingham in June 1392, the post of mayor of London was dissolved by Richard II, who had the support of 24 leading commoners, including the important mercer Richard ('Dick') Whittington, who became an alderman of London in March 1393. Whittington then served under Dallingridge, for on 25 June 1392: 'Having got rid of the name of mayor, the king appointed as the first warden of the city a knight called Sir Edward Dallingridge.'

Fulfilling the role of Warden of the City of London shows Sir Edward was fit and active. Yet he had only a year to live before his death in August 1393 aged around 47. He was succeeded by his son Sir John, also a courtier, MP and royal ambassador. In 1406, Sir John married Alice, daughter of Sir John Beauchamp of Powick, Worcestershire and widow of Thomas Boteler of Sudeley, Gloucestershire. He died childless in 1408.

Castle and home

Bodiam Castle wasn't a vision of past glories for a retired old soldier, for Sir Edward Dallingridge never retired; he was not merely a soldier, nor particularly old. However, some believe it was a visible demonstration of the lordly patriotism of a leading warrior, a role that elevated him to the rank of courtier. Perhaps this fortified residence offered a defence against English rebels, or French raiders, or even provided a refuge from urban plague. Then again, it may have been all of those things, for Bodiam seems at once the epitome of a castle, yet equally a neatly-designed courtyard house. It is small for a fortress, but it carries the machinery of defence and copious space for the provisions necessary to withstand a siege. To better understand its role in this turbulent age, and explain some of its anomalies, we might first ask this: what could such a medieval castle represent to the medieval mind?

The medieval idea of a castle

A medieval castle was essentially a fortified residence or site, the term adopted from the Latin *'castellum'* for a small Roman fort, a diminutive of *'castra'* for military camp. English castles are often explained foremost as military solutions for their patrons' personal defence.

A brief history of the English castle

The arrival in 1066 of William the Conqueror brought Norman castles to England. Often, at first, they consisted of timber palisades defending a motte (mound) and bailey (lower, domestic forecourt). As the new administration grew fully established in the following decades, castles evolved into massive stone keeps surrounded by defended curtain walls.

The twelfth century saw great innovations in castle design, especially when the crusades after 1096 demanded protection for troops and pilgrims in remote and hostile lands near Jerusalem. In the thirteenth century, round towers became standard to deflect heavy catapulted missiles, while concentric rings of curtain walls and complex entrance gates called barbicans provided layers of defences for archers. The use of gunpowder in the fourteenth and fifteenth centuries coincided with a decreased threat of invasion, whereupon castles became country houses with large windows that would have been vulnerable to attack.

There is truth in this brief history of English castles. But functionalism is only one way of seeing them. Castles weren't consistent in their design and sophistication; threats varied regionally, locally and personally – some builders were royal, others nobles or knights. Hence, each building must be seen as a response to particular circumstances. As importantly, they were never purely defensive, but were lived in and served to project ideas about the owners' identity and values. So, medieval perceptions about what castles represented must precede our consideration of practical fortification. And to the medieval mind the idea of the castle brought a host of associations that aren't obvious to us today.

Above Corfe Castle in Dorset has the classic early medieval combination of towering stone keep and curtain walls below

The Virgin Mary

Many intellectual concepts in medieval culture were drawn from, or related to, the Bible, and castles were no exception. The Virgin Mary was associated with the descriptions of fortifications in the Song of Solomon.

Thy neck is like the tower of David builded for an armoury, whereon there hang a thousand bucklers, all shields of mighty men.

Song of Solomon, 4:4

This association with Mary was made because, as the mother of Christ, she was deemed to be impregnable except to God. Her womb, which received the holy spirit by which Christ was understood to have been conceived, was symbolised by the *hortus conclusus* (enclosed garden). Medieval depictions consistently showed her within such a fertile garden, which was bounded by a crenellated wall, sometimes with arrow-loops; often, the entrance was a tower, draped with shields. To soldiers across Europe, Mary was the great protectress, and medieval builders manifested this idea in the design of gates and defences.

Right above **The Madonna and Child were often depicted in an enclosed garden surrounded by a battlemented wall**

Right below **The round towers of Corfe's Outer Gatehouse were designed to deflect missiles**

Heraldry at Bodiam

Bodiam Castle displays original heraldic shields in two locations: the Gatehouse and Postern Tower. On the Gatehouse the heraldry is arrayed as an inverted 'T', like the top of a cross, with Dallingridge's arms placed centrally. The ensemble is surmounted by his tournament helm featuring a unicorn, this chosen position representing its importance to Dallingridge's identity. The unicorn was symbolic of Christ – a pure creature hunted for its blood, and when shown in Paradise in lieu of Christ, its horn usually points to the Virgin's womb. When Dallingridge fought with this device, its connotation was clear: he was a warrior willing to sacrifice his blood in imitation of Christ. To either side of his arms are the shields of his extended families: Wardieu and Radyngen. This bottom row might be seen as the temporal realm of heraldry. Following the same sense of priority, his previous relationship to Sir Robert Knollys is shown on the Postern Tower, the rear of the building where Knollys's arms are set between two blank shields, while the Knollys ram's head is set above. All these devices are likely to have been painted.

Right Coats of arms feature prominently on the Gatehouse

The castle and the cult of Mary

As a Commissioner of the household of Richard II, Sir Edward Dallingridge was deeply acquainted with current court arts. So perhaps the first thing to understand about Bodiam Castle is that in Dallingridge's era the Virgin Mary and her realm were intrinsically associated with the idea of an English castle. Her spiritual protection probably formed part of Bodiam's assumed impregnability, beyond its practical stone and mortar. This concept was expressed in the heraldry (see box) and the lost arts of the castle's chapel, the only part of the building to break symmetry and call attention to itself.

Above In the Wilton Diptych in the National Gallery, Richard II is shown praying to the Virgin Mary for the protection of England

Building Bodiam Castle

The River Rother was diverted by Dallingridge as part of his landscaping of the site

No building accounts survive to explain the stages of Bodiam Castle's construction, nor diaries, letters or other personal insights into the Dallingridge family's priorities. The building is our principal witness.

Date

Henry Wardieu, who was lord of Bodiam Manor in 1314, settled his estates on his son Master Nicholas, who, with his brother Richard, was holding Bodiam in 1320. Nicholas was dead by September 1330, leaving a son, John. A fine but damaged brass in Bodiam church identifiable only from its heraldry as a member of the Wardieu family, is likely to represent John Wardieu, whose daughter and heiress, Elizabeth, married Sir Edward Dallingridge in 1363 and through whom they inherited the estate on John's death in 1377.

Documents accounting for the origins of the castle consist of Dallingridge's licence for his fair and market in 1383, implying an intention to settle here; the 1385 licence to crenellate, which may signal the completion of construction; and a licence to divert the River Rother to his watermill in 1386, when the site was being landscaped.

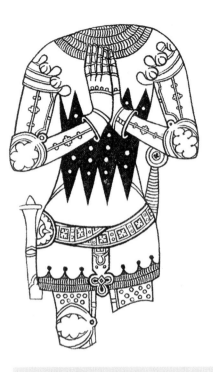

Above The remains of a tomb brass in Bodiam church of a member of the Wardieu family – probably John Wardieu, the father-in-law of the builder of the castle

The Licence to crenellate Bodiam, 1385
The King to all men to whom etc. greeting. Know that of our special grace we have granted and given license on behalf of ourselves and our heirs, in so far as in us lies, to our beloved and faithful Edward Dallingridge Knight, that he may strengthen with a wall of stone and lime, and crenellate and may construct and make into a castle his manor house of Bodyham, near the sea, in the County of Sussex, for the defence of the adjacent country, and the resistance to our enemies, and may hold his aforesaid house so strengthened and crenellated and made into a castle for himself and his heirs for ever, without let or hindrance of ourselves or our heirs, or of any of our agents whatsoever. In witness of which etc. The King at Westminster 20 October.

Setting

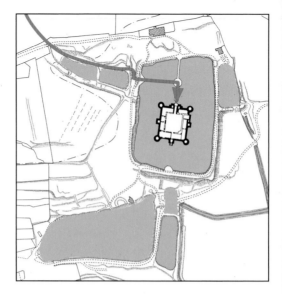

The way in which guests were received onto a late medieval estate was of considerable social – and particularly chivalric – importance.

The degree of ceremony with which they were conducted into a castle reflected the visitors' rank. It was time-honoured courtesy that the most honoured guests would be joined on their approach – sometimes for long distances – by their host. The castle might be admired at various points from a distance, and the final approach to the castle across the bridge was the culmination of this ceremonial progress. What did they see at Bodiam?

The situation of Bodiam on a spur presented an impressive aspect when approaching from the south; better still, from the east along the Rother from the coast. The large windows of the chapel and principal apartments face this direction, offering undoubtedly impressive vistas.

The castle's situation at the foot of a scarp enabled the construction of a terraced earthwork, once known as the Gun Garden, to its north. Archaeological evidence, including its alignment with the northern stretch of the moat, suggests it was built at the same time as the castle, provided a viewing platform for a garden known as a 'pleasaunce'. To the north of this terrace, the medieval house on the 'Court Lodge' site may well have retained its ancillary buildings for use by the castle: stables, barns and the like. The manor courts were held at Court Lodge until at least 1443.

The principal approach to the castle by road was on the west side, where a string of ponds – not a road or track – was aligned with the octagonal barbican. (Opposite, to the east and seemingly aligned, is another water garden feature called the 'Little Moat').These more immediate areas of earthworks and gardens framed the building as an extension of the residence itself. Today, the complex series of ponds is seen as dry earthworks for most of the year. Water gardens and fishponds may well have emulated the biblical descriptions of the Virgin Mary (see p.15). In peacetime, their planting could be enjoyed, while they offered power for mills and a perennial stock of fish for the table, though trawling ponds was hardly practical in times of siege.

Leeds Castle and Kenilworth established water gardens at much the same time as Bodiam. Shirburn also had some, but the fashion wasn't limited to England. At Hesdin in Picardy the Duke of Burgundy contrived a watery landscape for amusement with real and mechanical menageries, widely seen by ambassadors from across Europe.

Opposite The original
route to the castle

This page The castle in
its setting today

Shape

Bodiam Castle is built on an apparently symmetrical plan.

This was not novel, for some of Edward I's Welsh castles built from the 1290s were laid out symmetrically with round towers at the corners, flanking central gatehouses. Bodiam's symmetry was probably typical of the late fourteenth century, when the English drew much inspiration from French design, as well as native buildings.

The basic concept of Bodiam is a rectangular courtyard house of integrated ranges set neatly within a curtain wall. Unlike the Welsh castles, conceived with service and accommodation buildings clinging to the interior faces of their curtain walls, Edward III's rebuilding of the Upper Ward of Windsor Castle after 1356 established a united ensemble. This comprised a northern range of hall and chapel united by a regularised façade, with lodgings opposite, to the south.

The surveyor for Windsor Castle was William Wykeham, Bishop of Winchester. Bishops were great builders, and Wykeham himself re-used the Windsor blueprint for New College, Oxford (from 1379). But the knight was a still more obvious type of courtier to absorb the lessons of fortification, residence and court style. Bodiam's closest English equivalent prior to 1385 is Shirburn Castle in Oxfordshire, which Warrin

Left above The French castle of Derval was owned by Dallingridge's commander Sir Robert Knollys and has many similarities to Bodiam

Left below Shirburn Castle in Oxfordshire is closely comparable to Bodiam: symmetrical, with round towers at each corner

de Lisle was licensed to crenellate in 1377, but is much changed. The moated French castle of Derval belonging to Dallingridge's sponsor Robert Knollys is strikingly similar to Shirburn, and even more so to Bodiam. Derval featured not only a symmetrical rectangular exterior with round turrets, but a barbican reached by a 90-degree dog-leg, as at Bodiam. Having been built in occupied territory at acute risk of French aggression, Derval was a defensible fortress. So it is particularly intriguing that Knollys's arms are shown prominently at Bodiam.

Castles such as Derval, and the accommodation expected by the court after the example of Windsor, are likely to have influenced a class of knights involved in the opening forays of the Hundred Years War. When the young Richard II took to the throne in 1377, the power vacuum of a royal minority was filled by the interests of the aristocracy, as usual. This generation jostled for favour and elevation on account of their established prowess as defenders of the realm, and may have built castles to an unusual degree.

The concept for any great medieval masonry building like Bodiam was given over to master masons. They offered a 'master-plan', but then usually delegated detailed design issues to supervised subordinates. Principal amongst these advisory architects was Henry Yevele (c.1325–1400), the head of the King's Works, who led the creation of Canterbury's Westgate, which much resembles Bodiam, as well as work at the Tower of London in 1379. Yevele then supervised Cooling Castle in Kent, the fortified residence of John of Cobham. Bodiam was built at the same time as two other Yevele projects: Arundel Castle in Sussex (c.1380) and Saltwood Castle in Kent (c.1385–94). Bodiam's confidently orchestrated details such as gun-loops, hexagonal tower-chambers and vaulting with ring-bosses all suggest an exceptionally competent designer at ease with the military court manner, and its design may have involved Yevele. But – contrary to appearances – Bodiam wasn't constructed in one phase.

Above Cooling Castle in Kent is also similar to Bodiam

Layout

The castle as completed comprises a single courtyard within a curtain wall 2.2 metres thick at the base, rising 13.15 metres from the stone retaining wall within its moat. It was built in four main layers of construction, as revealed by horizontal joints in its masonry.

The digging of the moat necessarily pre-dated the construction of the castle itself, as the curtain walls and towers were laid by builders with access to their external faces. Between those two phases – moat and present castle – was an early masonry structure of about 9 × 5.7 metres on the east range of the castle, its walls about 0.9 metres thick, though the east wall was thicker at about 1.7 metres. It was extended north with a second cell. That this substantial mass was then incorporated in the east curtain wall of the present castle, against the line of the moat, suggests this may be the truncated start of a slightly earlier house with varied ranges.

Left Even the small spiral stairs are decorated with battlements

Opposite above This large window lit the Great Hall

Opposite below One of the narrow lancet windows

The plan is arranged with distinct apartments of self-contained accommodation. The northern gatehouse is aligned with the Screens Passage of the Great Hall to the south. This hall stood between Dallingridge's kitchens and the private apartments, probably with unique access to the chapel.

Windows

Most of the external windows are small lancets or square-headed openings. All the windows on the west and north elevations, seen from rising ground, are of this form. By contrast, the east elevation, and the east end of the south elevation, seen from the marshes and meadows of the River Rother below, have some larger windows. On the east, a large three-light traceried window lit the projecting chapel, with two-light lancets to each floor of the principal apartments to its south. The hall, at the east end of the south elevation, had a large two-light mullion-and-transom window at the high end.

As revised, the completed castle features round (drum) towers on the corners (about 8.7 metres diameter), with square towers at the centre of the west and east sides, a principal gatehouse with portcullises at the centre of the north side, and a secondary, postern gate-tower at the centre of the south side.

The Gatehouse and Postern Tower are crenellated and machicolated; the other towers and wall walks have, or had, crenellations with very wide merlons. Those from the wall-walks are largely lost, and those to the towers are mainly nineteenth- and early twentieth-century restorations using stone found on site. The theme of crenellation was continued at a decorative scale in the diminutive parapets of the small flat roofs over the stair turrets, and in the miniature battlements to the caps of the hexagonal chimneys. These now mostly survive on the towers, but originally also enlivened the profile of the wall walks (a pair survives on the east side).

Exploring the Castle

Sir Edward and his guests would have arrived at Bodiam across a water garden and over drawbridges.

The Octagon and Barbican

The Approach

The medieval experience is lost, but, from the polygonal bulwark at the north-west corner of the moat, we can still appreciate the impressive mass of this fortress-residence.

The Octagon

In the middle of the north arm of the moat is the Octagon. It was originally reached across a bridge, the foundations surviving beneath the water. We now enter via a northern bridge, a route established by the early eighteenth century.

The Barbican

On a rectangular island to the south of the Octagon is the Barbican, the remains of a fortified outbuilding that protected the main Gatehouse. This two-storey structure was occupied by a guard and had its own portcullis.

The Gatehouse

The Gatehouse is a fine design with severe, massive walls and projecting machicolations featuring a crenellated parapet that could conceal archers. Beyond mere appearances, it features several integrated lines of defence. Bodiam was built during the early development of hand-held cannons, and the Gatehouse contains gun-loops from which to fire them. These features are often considered as only for show, but the non-combatant may underestimate the danger of exploded hailshot at close quarters.

The Gatehouse provided self-contained accommodation, probably for a constable, who was responsible for security. It had three portcullis gates, the original outermost grille of iron-clad oak remaining, and there were also two sets of timber gates hung on iron pintles (hinge pins), one of which sets was restored around 1830. The vault above features ring-bosses, which are typical of military and court buildings of the period.

Above Ring-bosses, or murder-holes, in the vaulted ceiling of the Gatehouse, through which missiles could be dropped on attackers

Left The entrance gate and portcullis

Below A gun-loop in the Gatehouse, from which hand-held weapons could be fired

The Courtyard

Today, the courtyard presents a bewildering array of irregular, ruined walls, where once there were neat façades of stone-built lodgings. Interpreting the layout requires some speculation, but the essential framework remains clear.

The Screens Passage

Straight ahead, on the opposite (south) side of the central courtyard, is the Screens Passage of the Great Hall. This passage divided the house between the service end (west, right) and the principal lodgings (east, left).

The Postern Tower

Beyond the Screens Passage are the vault and external arch of the Postern Tower, the 'tradesmen's entrance' once used for delivering goods, via a drawbridge. This does, however, bear the arms of Knollys which suggests it may have provided an alternative entrance. It also once had a portcullis.

Below The three doorways in the Screens Passage once led to the Buttery, Kitchen and Pantry

Opposite The Postern Tower

The Kitchen

From the Screens Passage, the Kitchen was reached through the central of three rebuilt stone arches into a passage flanked by storage rooms. In a typical arrangement, the outer arches led to a pantry, for bread, on the south, and a buttery – for drinks (after *'bouteille'*), on the north. Above them were lodgings. At the western end of the passage came the serving place lit by opposing windows. The servery hatch to the Kitchen was spanned by a large beam that fitted into the sockets. The Kitchen itself is clearly identified by a huge roasting hearth in the south wall. On the north side a second hearth is seen with bread or pastry ovens set within an inserted wall that may be original or slightly later.

The South-West Tower

From the Kitchen, steps lead down into the south-western turret to a pool, probably fed by a spring. There is no other evidence for a well, and this supply of once fresh water was ideally positioned. The upper levels of this tower comprise fine accommodation suitable for a kitchen steward (a valued role), rising to a dovecote with nesting boxes.

The Forme of Cury [cookery]

The Forme of Cury is the earliest-known English recipe book, written by the courtiers of King Richard II, about 1390. Their aim was to '... techith a man for to make commune potages and commune meetis for howshold as they shold be made craftly and holsomly. Aftirward it techith for to make curious potages & meetes and sotiltees for alle maner of States bothe hye and lowe.' The book lists swans, herons, bitterns – all then common in Sussex. One recipe is for sausage of the sort that may have been served to the Dallingridges' guests.

Pygg in sawse sawge

'Take Pigges yskaldid and quarter hem and seeth hem in water and salt, take hem and lat hem kele, take persel sawge and grynde it with brede and zolkes of ayrenn harde ysode. temper it up with vyneger sum what thyk. and, lay the Pygges in a vessell. and the sewe onoward and serue it forth.'

Left below The roasting hearth in the Kitchen

Right below The pool in the South-West Tower would have supplied fresh water to the castle

The Great Hall

To the east of the Screens Passage, the Great Hall was once entered through a timber screen, typically with a loft. Now roofless, the hall was used for the daily communal meals of the household. The servants sat at forms (backless benches), with tables set lengthways along the hall. The Dallingridges were provided with a stepped dais at the eastern end, so that – in principle – they sat facing the Screens Passage, supervising the entire room, while expensive metalware was displayed behind them on 'cup-boards'. But in practice, many patrons retreated to Parlours or Great Chambers to eat. The size of the kitchens here suggests they may have used the Parlour for important receptions, while retinues ate in the hall.

The Private Apartments

It was typical of medieval great houses that the 'high' end of the hall led into the main private apartments. The dais stair led through 90 degrees to the Parlour, the first of the withdrawing spaces of increasing privacy and richness from the Great Chamber to the patrons' bedchambers. At Bodiam, they occupied the eastern range set over a basement with bedchamber suites at ground and first floors, as can be seen by the fireplaces.

The crenellations on the first-floor chimneypiece indicate that this was Sir Edward's apartment. Royal apartments came to be stacked, separating king from queen, but this was ceremonial: we might expect Edward and Elizabeth to have customarily shared a bedchamber.

The occupants of this upper apartment were provided with a warmed room with a latrine. They also had a small, private oratory and windows overlooking the altar within the adjacent double-height Chapel.

Below Reconstruction of the internal courtyard

1. Private apartments
2. Great Hall
3. Screens Passage
4. Postern Tower
5. Kitchen

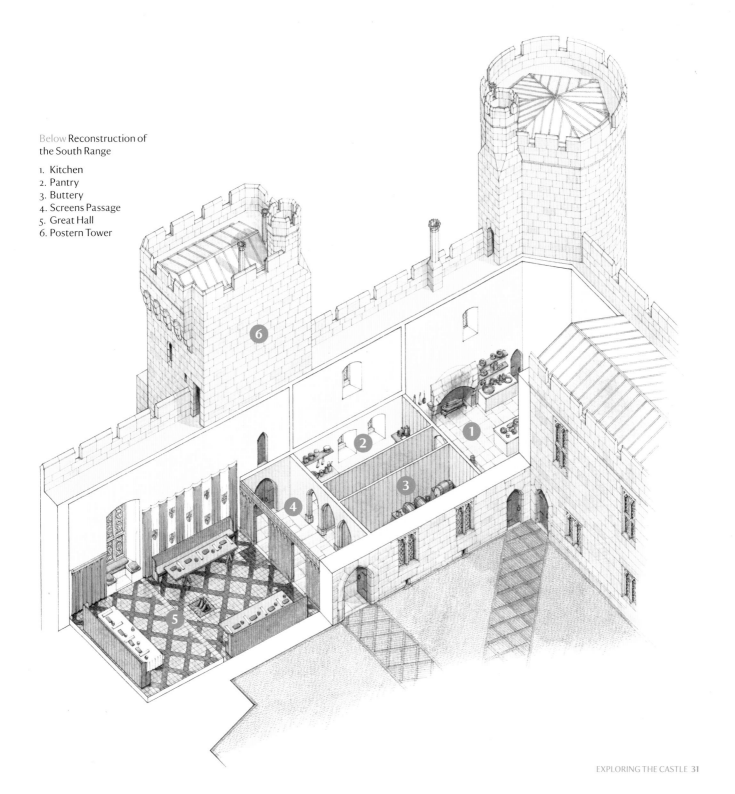

Below Reconstruction of
the South Range

1. Kitchen
2. Pantry
3. Buttery
4. Screens Passage
5. Great Hall
6. Postern Tower

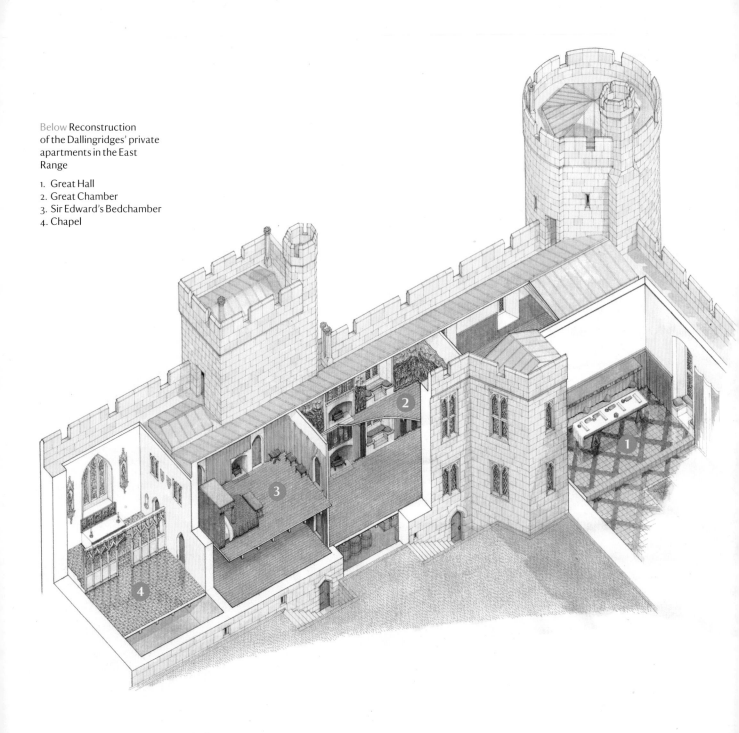

Below Reconstruction
of the Dallingridges' private
apartments in the East
Range

1. Great Hall
2. Great Chamber
3. Sir Edward's Bedchamber
4. Chapel

The Chapel

The Chapel's main entrance was from the courtyard, up steps to a space paved in cream and green Flemish tiles and divided by a fine screen carved from chalk. Remains can be seen of the aumbry and piscina, for storing and washing communion vessels. Here, we must ask how Dallingridge's identification with the Christian unicorn over the main Gatehouse was developed. A crucifixion is amongst probable imagery, possibly in stained glass in the tripartite window (repaired by Cubitt), flanked by the Dallingridges praying. Or perhaps this castle featured the militant St George (or St Michael or St Margaret), or the Virgin Mary with her promise of redemption. This much is informed speculation.

The North-East and North-West Ranges

The North-East Range offered flexibly arranged guest lodgings, separated from access to the wall-walks. Views to the water gardens and terrace were undoubtedly important qualities of these lodgings. The same can be said for the North-West Range, which may have been second-class guest lodgings.

Right above **The Chapel window**

Right **The East Range**

The West Range

The West Range is the most archaeologically puzzling. Adjacent to the Kitchen, it was a service range with flue-containing walls that are mostly original. The tiles show where there were charcoal braziers that may have served a brewhouse – important in an age when most people drank weak ale.

There are many patches of later repair and rebuilding, but evidence remains for a staircase to an upper floor, which was later strengthened. So it seems this was third-class accommodation transformed into storage, as the way the castle was used shifted in the later Middle Ages.

Later History

The Gatehouse harbours extensive historic graffiti that reveal centuries of occupation and visiting.

Written upon the walls

For anyone visiting Bodiam Castle today, the graffiti inscriptions carved into its stones offer fascinating insights. The area around the gatehouse contains hundreds of clearly visible inscriptions, stretching back many centuries. The majority of these date from relatively recent times, and reflect the growth of the site as an early tourist attraction. One was created by James Bryan, of the 35th Regiment of Foot, who visited the castle in 1818, whilst his unit was temporarily stationed at Brighton. A few decades later, in 1850, Jane Hook and Ann Pratt sent a great deal of time neatly and precisely cutting their names into the doorway of the Postern. More recently still, you can make out inscriptions from the Second World War, when parts of the castle were used by the Home Guard. However, if you look closely at the stones of the castle, you may stumble upon inscriptions left by those people who lived and worked here during the later Middle Ages, such as 'Johannes' (John) who neatly carved his name into a door surround in the upper floor of the gatehouse.

Witch marks

Alongside these early graffiti inscriptions are many marks left by the medieval masons who built Bodiam in the late fourteenth century, giving us many insights into the actual construction process and the people who worked here. Perhaps most intriguingly are the large number of symbols for ritual protection, more commonly known as 'Witch Marks', that have been identified around almost every entrance and window in the castle. Designed to 'ward off' evil influences, these reinforce the idea that for the medieval occupants of the castle, strong defences required more than battlements and gun-loops. At Bodiam the history of the castle really is written upon the walls.

archaeologist Matthew Champion

When Sir Edward Dallingridge died in the summer of 1393, he was succeeded by his son Sir John, also a courtier, MP and royal ambassador. In 1406 Sir John married Alice Beauchamp, who was the widow of Thomas Boteler of Sudeley, Gloucestershire, and held the family seat of Sudeley. Sir John died childless two years later. His estates passed to Alice for her lifetime, entailed at her death successively to his cousins Richard and William, sons of Sir Edward's younger brother Walter. Alice was chatelaine of Bodiam until her death, and Bodiam seems to have been her principal seat.

The Lewknors

Richard Dallingridge inherited Bodiam Castle in 1443, and died childless in 1471, having outlived his brother. His estates, including Bodiam Castle, then passed to his sister Philippa, and through her second husband, Sir Thomas Lewknor, to his descendants.

The Lewknor family were large landowners in Sussex, well-established elsewhere. Bodiam, considered an unhealthy location, seems at best to have become a secondary seat. Sir Thomas Lewknor's son Sir Roger I (d.1478, described as 'of Dedisham') inherited, and is recorded as the castle's owner in 1473. His heir was another Sir Thomas Lewknor (1456–1484), described as 'of Trotton'. Sir Thomas Lewknor II supported the Lancastrian cause and took part in the Duke of Buckingham's rebellion in 1483, soon after Richard III came to the throne. A commission was issued to the king's men in the county to 'besiege the castle of Bodyham which the rebels

Left The mutilated torso of the tomb effigy of Sir John Dallingridge, the son of the builder of Bodiam. He died in 1408

have seized'. The castle appears to have been surrendered peacefully and a Yeoman of the Crown, Nicholas Rigby, was appointed constable in 1484 'with the keeping of the park', set to the south of the castle and mill-pond.

During the age of the Dissolution of the Monasteries, when monastic properties were parcelled up, in 1543 Sir Roger Lewknor divided the estate between his daughters. In 1645, the by now reunited castle and its lands were sold to Nathaniel Powell of Ewhurst, a lawyer and ironmaster and leader of a consortium of investors, and within six years Powell was sole owner of the castle and immediate surroundings. He saw the property as a commercial asset.

Antiquarians

Sir Thomas Webster, Baronet, bought the estate in 1723. Webster owned vast holdings in Essex, Surrey and Sussex, and two years previously had bought Battle Abbey with 8,000 acres.

The Ewhurst estate that included Bodiam extended to 800 acres, while Webster also bought Robertsbridge Abbey with 1,100 acres in 1726. So he owned three significant medieval monuments, suggesting that he appreciated buildings of this period. In 1737 Nathaniel Buck made an antiquarian engraving, the first to show Bodiam in detail. He presents a ruin, with plants growing from the towers, with a northern causeway already in place as an entrance to the main gatehouse.

Bodiam was settled on Sir Thomas's son Whistler Webster in 1733, who succeeded in 1751. When he died in 1779, it rapidly descended to his grandson Sir Godfrey Webster, who was no friend of ancient monuments. Nonetheless, a growing tide of antiquarian interest brought a series of drawings by Grimm in 1784, showing vegetable plots in the inner courtyard making the most of a walled garden with plentiful water.

Above Nathiel Buck's 1737 engraving of Bodiam

A frustrated 'castle hunter'

'This castle belongs to Sir Godfrey Webster, who has locked up the gate leading to the interior of the square and from narrowness of possession does not allow a key to any neighbour; tho, surely a proper inhabitant would secure and preserve it and get a livelyhood (or at least much support) from us, castle hunters. So I could only walk around the little lake that washes the building and adds much to the curiosity and safety of the building.'

Lord Torrington, 1788

At some point during the late eighteenth or early nineteenth centuries the Barbican's east wall, passage and vault collapsed or were taken down, leaving only the fragment on the west side. It is possible that Bodiam kept prisoners of the Napoleonic wars at this time.

Webster eventually sold Bodiam Castle in 1829 with just 25 acres (62 hectares) of surrounding land to John ('Mad Jack') Fuller, the famously eccentric squire of Brightling, and a Tory MP. His purchase was widely thought to have been made to prevent the castle from being dismantled, and while he contrived a picturesquely wooded parkland setting, his repairs included 'paveing with cowpoo' and hanging oak doors in the Postern Tower. More substantial work would soon be needed.

Above 'Mad Jack' Fuller, who built a tower at Brightling, from which he is said to have observed his repairs to Bodiam six miles away

Left The interior of ivy-clad Bodiam in 1782, when it was being used to grow vegetables and contained large trees

Repair and restoration

From 1864 to 1917, George Cubitt owned a castle in rapid decay. He commissioned a survey by J. Tavenor Parry to inform the masonry repairs carried out by the local schoolmaster Charles Thompson.

Cubitt rebuilt much of the capping of the main gatehouse and south-west tower. Though he left trees and ivy in the courtyard, he claimed to have '... put it into thorough repair without any alteration and instituted a small payment for admission...' The tourist trade had arrived, and Cubitt gave Bodiam the Castle Hotel.

Curzon the conservationist

When the former Viceroy of India, Lord Curzon, 1st Marquess of Kedleston, arrived in 1917, he disposed of all but 50 acres (124 hectares) of Bodiam Castle's parkland. As the owner of Tattershall Castle in Lincolnshire, in 1911 he had

Left Lord Curzon, who repaired the castle and presented it to the National Trust

Below left The foundations of two medieval bridges to the castle were revealed in 1919, when Curzon drained the moat. It was drained again in 1970, when a thorough investigation took place

Right The ivy-covered Barbican as it was before being restored by Lord Curzon

stopped the export of its fireplaces and having reinstalled them, set about reforming heritage protection. This resulted in the 1913 Ancient Monuments Consolidation and Amendment Act 1913, which brought about the Ancient Monuments Board. Concentrating on the castle itself, he then began a campaign of study and repair led by the architect William Weir, who undid much of Cubitt's work. Curzon was a paradoxical character. Though he sensitively analysed the fabric of the building, he introduced concrete. Plans were drawn up to turn Bodiam into a residence, though no progress was made, as he 'desisted from what would have been an interesting architectural experiment, but might easily have degenerated into an archaeological crime.'

Curzon placed the future care of Bodiam into the hands of the National Trust after his death in 1925. Almost a century on, it has lost none of its power to fascinate.

Ancient and modern: The pill-box

On your way back to the car-park, turn aside to look at the brick pill-box, a relic of twentieth-century war built in the shadow of the medieval castle.

After the fall of France in May 1940, Britain was suddenly and unexpectedly faced with the threat of a German invasion. General Sir Edmund Ironside, Commander-in-Chief of the Home Forces, decided on a policy of layered defence. Inland, he created several lines of defence to slow down the German advance, using natural features where possible.

The Bodiam pill-box was part of a defensive line along the River Rother, a natural tank barrier. It is built of brick and reinforced concrete, and commands the bridge over the river 300 metres to the west. The pill-box comprises two chambers, the principal one for a six-pounder Hotchkiss anti-tank gun, and an annexe for machine guns. It was manned by ten men from the Canadian Army and then by the Home Guard, probably until 1944, when the threat of invasion had disappeared.

Left The pill-box